Some animals have shells. Under
the shell is the animal's soft body.

1

Limpets, mussels, clams and whelks are shellfish. They can be found in rock pools.

They cling onto rocks or lie hidden in the weed at the bottom of the pool.

When shellfish die, the shells are left empty. You can collect the shells.

Tortoises and terrapins have shells with patterns on them.

A tortoise or terrapin
can tuck its head, legs
and tail into its shell if
a predator comes along.

Crabs and lobsters have shells which are a sort of hard skin.

A lobster has a jointed shell. It flaps its tail to swim.

As the lobster gets bigger, its shell splits. The fresh shell is soft to begin with, but it soon hardens.

There are lots of different sorts of crabs. Some are good at swimming, some live inland, and some have long thin legs.

Hermit crabs do not have shells.
They look for empty shells to live in.

Whenever a hermit crab
gets bigger, it has to
hunt for a bigger shell.

A snail has a coiled shell.
A slug has a funny sort of
shell that you cannot see.

Its shell is hidden in its body!